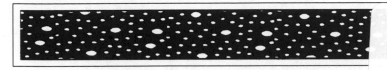

WILD ABOUT
SALADS

BY MARIE BIANCO

BARRON'S

New York • London • Toronto • Sydney

All inquiries should be addressed to:
Barron's Educational Series, Inc.
250 Wireless Boulevard
Hauppauge, New York 11788

Library of Congress Catalog Card No. 88-7714
International Standard Book No. 0-8120-4092-9

Library of Congress Cataloging in Publication Data

Bianco, Marie.
    Wild about salads.

    Includes index.
    1. Salads.   I. Title.
TX740.B52 1989   641.8'3   88-7714
ISBN 0-8120-4092-9

Design by Milton Glaser, Inc.
Color photographs by Matthew Klein
Francine Matalon-Degni, photo stylist
Andrea Swenson, food stylist
Photo 1 opposite page 16: server courtesy of Oneida, Ltd.
Photo 6 opposite page 33: servers courtesy of Oneida, Ltd.
Photo 10 opposite page 49: fork courtesy of Oneida, Ltd.
Photo 11 opposite page 56: plate courtesy of Ceramica
Photo 14 opposite page 65: bowl and plate courtesy of Ceramica; flatware, Oneida, Ltd.
Photo 16 opposite page 81: fork courtesy of Oneida, Ltd.

Printed and bound in Hong Kong

9012 4900 987654321

CONTENTS

INTRODUCTION

An old Roman adage advises that it takes four people to make the perfect salad. There should be a spendthrift pouring the oil, a miser adding the vinegar, a wise man doing the seasoning and a madman tossing it all together.

It is generally believed that the word "salad" is derived from the Latin herba salate, meaning salted greens. The earliest salads were probably fresh greens plucked from the landscape which the Romans munched with a simple sprinkling of salt.

In the past few years no other menu category has had so many new and innovative changes as the salad course. People are eating lighter and more wisely, and a salad combining large amounts of vegetables with small amounts of protein presents a healthier meal than a hamburger and French fries.

Today's leafy salads are a collection of greens: tart arugula, bitter radicchio, satiny endive, assertive spinach, peppery watercress, baby lettuces, nutty mâche. Truly inventive salad makers add a splash of vibrant color with an edible flower garnish of nasturtium or pansies. Perhaps the biggest innovations are the warm/cold salads—combinations of warm seafood, poultry or meat atop dressed chilled greens or pasta, a

*contrast of temperature, texture and tastes. Cold pasta is no
longer limited to macaroni salad; mayonnaise and showy fruit
salads are bright and cheerful.*

*The art of salad making should spark the imagination.
The salad should be as pleasing to the eye as it is to the palate. A
humdrum salad, like a wedge of iceberg lettuce covered with
bottled orange dressing, does nothing for the appetite—but the
same iceberg lettuce, anointed with fruity olive oil and a dash of
balsamic vinegar and decorated with an array of fresh
vegetables, can be a collage of colors and taste.*

*Presentation is important. The classic salad bowl is
wood, but a glass dish allows more visibility, especially for tossed
salads. An alternative is the composed salad, what the French
call* salade composée: *attractive ingredients formally
arranged on a platter or on individual dishes.*

*When I think of making a salad, I like to have a surprise
in every bite, so don't be afraid to experiment with ingredients.*

CONVERSION TABLES

The weights and measure in the lists of ingredients and cooking instructions for each recipe are in both U.S. and metric units.

LIQUID MEASURES

The Imperial cup is considerably larger than the U. S. cup. Use the following table to convert to Imperial liquid units.

AMERICAN CUP (in book)	IMPERIAL CUP (adjusts to)
¼ cup	4 tablespoons
⅓ cup	5 tablespoons
½ cup	8 tablespoons
⅔ cup	¼ pint
¾ cup	¼ pint + 2 tablespoons
1 cup	¼ pint + 6 tablespoons
1¼ cups	½ pint
1½ cups	½ pint + 4 tablespoons
2 cups	¾ pint
2½ cups	1 pint
3 cups	1½ pints
4 cups	1½ pints + 4 tablespoons
5 cups	2 pints

Note: The Australian and Canadian cup measures 250 mL and is only slightly larger than the U. S. cup, which is 236mL. Cooks in Australia and Canada can follow the exact measurements given in the recipes, using either the U. S. or metric measures.

SOLID MEASURES

British and Australian cooks measure more items by weight. Here are approximate equivalents for basic items in the book.

	U. S. Customary	Imperial
Cheese (grated)	½ cup	2 oz.
	1 cup	4 oz.
Herbs (fresh chopped)	¼ cup	¼ oz.
Nuts (chopped)	¼ cup	1 oz.
	½ cup	2 oz.
	1 cup	4 oz.
Raisins	¼ cup	1½ oz.
	½ cup	3 oz.
	1 cup	6 oz.
Rice	½ cup	4 oz.
	1 cup	8 oz.
	2 cup	16 oz.
Vegetables (chopped)	½ cup	2 oz.
	1 cup	4 oz.
	2 cups	8 oz.

SALAD MAIN DISHES

The problem of whether to serve a salad before or after the main course has just been solved—make a salad the entree and everybody is happy. Each of these salads is especially suited to warm weather, and needs only a good bread, a suitable beverage and a dessert to fill out the meal.

VITELLO TONNATO

SERVES 6

INGREDIENTS

2 tablespoons olive oil
2 tablespoons white wine
1 tablespoon chopped fresh
thyme, or 1 teaspoon dried
salt and pepper to taste
2 veal tenderloins
7-ounce (200-g) can tuna packed
in water, drained
¼ cup (60 mL) dry white wine
2 tablespoons fresh lime juice
2 anchovy fillets
1 cup (240 mL) mayonnaise,
preferably homemade
6 cups mesclun or a combination
of lettuces
2 ripe tomatoes, sliced
1 cup (115 g) black olives,
preferably Gaeta
(see note)
1 tablespoon capers, rinsed

Instead of using the customary veal roast, this version of veal with tuna sauce calls for grilled tenderloins.

Combine olive oil, wine, thyme, salt and pepper. Brush tenderloins with mixture and grill over hot coals for 10 minutes on each side. (They should be the barest pink in the center.) Cut into slices, then julienne.

To make dressing, combine tuna, wine, lime juice and anchovies in food processor or blender and blend until smooth. Add mayonnaise and mix well.

Arrange mesclun on serving platter. To assemble salad, arrange tomato slices, olives and veal over greens. Pour half the dressing over veal and garnish with capers. Serve remaining dressing on the side.

Note

Gaeta olives are small, purplish-black olives imported from Gaeta, Italy.

Pork tenderloins are tender and cook up fast. Try adding chunks of soaked mesquite to the hot coals for a smoky flavor.

Cook wild rice according to package directions. Rinse in cold water, drain and set aside.

Blanch sugar snap peas for 1 minute in boiling water. Drain; rinse in cold water. Drain and pat dry.

Grill pork tenderloin over hot coals for 10 minutes on each side (or to desired doneness), basting two or three times with olive oil. Slice pork diagonally.

To make dressing, whisk together ¾ cup olive oil, vinegar, dill, dill seed, salt and pepper.

Toss sugar snap peas, tomatoes, mushrooms, carrots and yellow pepper with half the dressing. Toss wild rice with remaining dressing. Place wild rice in center of serving dish. Arrange pork at one side and vegetables on the other. Garnish with fresh dill.

PORK AND WILD RICE SALAD

SERVES 6

INGREDIENTS

1 cup (150 g) wild rice
2 cups (230 g) sugar snap peas
1 pork tenderloin, about
1½ pounds (675 g)
olive oil for basting
¾ cup (180 mL) light olive oil
¼ cup (60 mL) cider vinegar
2 tablespoons chopped fresh dill
2 teaspoons dill seed
salt and pepper to taste
1 cup (115 g) cherry tomatoes
2 cups (230 g) sliced mushrooms
2 carrots, cooked, peeled,
julienned
1 large yellow bell pepper,
cut into strips
fresh dill

TURKEY SALAD VÉRONIQUE

SERVES 4

INGREDIENTS

2 cups (230 g) cooked rice, room temperature
2 cups (230 g) cubed cooked turkey
1 cup (115 g) seedless grapes, halved
½ cup (60 g) chopped celery
¼ cup (30 g) sliced scallions
½ cup (120mL) sour cream
½ cup (120 mL) mayonnaise
½ teaspoon celery seeds
1 teaspoon Dijon mustard
2 tablespoons dry white wine
¼ cup (30 g) chopped pecans
salad greens, washed and patted dry

This recipe makes use of leftover turkey breast, but it's just as good with roasted chicken.

In a medium bowl combine rice, turkey, grapes, celery and scallions. In a small bowl blend sour cream, mayonnaise, celery seeds, mustard and wine. Toss lightly with rice mixture. Serve on greens and sprinkle with pecans.

Couscous, made from ground semolina flour and water, is a North African favorite. Before the days of instant couscous, it was necessary to steam it for hours.

Combine orange juice, wine, honey, mustard, salt and pepper. Place in a shallow bowl and marinate chicken breasts in the refrigerator for 1 hour. Remove chicken and grill over hot coals 4 to 5 inches from heat for 15 minutes or until done, turning frequently and basting with any remaining marinade.

In a medium saucepan bring water and 1 tablespoon olive oil to boil. Add couscous, cover and set aside for 5 minutes. Remove cover, add 1 tablespoon olive oil, and fluff couscous with two forks. Repeat two or three times until couscous is room temperature and there are no lumps. Cook peas in lightly salted water for five minutes. Rinse under cold water and add to couscous with carrots, cilantro and walnuts. Add ½ cup olive oil and toss lightly. Season to taste with salt and pepper. Arrange couscous on platter and place chicken breasts on top.

GRILLED CHICKEN WITH COUSCOUS SALAD

SERVES 4

INGREDIENTS

¼ cup (60 mL) orange juice
¼ cup (60 mL) white wine
2 tablespoons honey
1 tablespoon Dijon mustard
Salt and pepper to taste
4 4-ounce (115-g) boneless,
skinless chicken breasts
2¼ cups (540 mL) water
2 tablespoons olive oil
1½ cups (350 g) quick-cooking
couscous
½ cup (60 g) green peas
1 cup (115 g) shredded carrot
2 tablespoons chopped cilantro
or parsley
½ cup (60 g) toasted walnuts,
chopped
½ cup (120 mL) olive oil

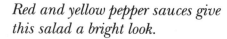

GRILLED CHICKEN WITH GRILLED VEGETABLES

SERVES 4

INGREDIENTS

4 boneless, skinless chicken
breast halves
approximately ½ cup olive oil
2 sprigs fresh tarragon
salt and pepper to taste
16 asparagus spears, blanched
3 minutes
2 medium zucchini, blanched 2
minutes, sliced diagonally
2 medium yellow crookneck
squash, blanched 2
minutes, sliced
diagonally
8 small new potatoes, cooked
10 minutes, cut in half
2 Japanese eggplants,
sliced diagonally
1 large sweet onion (such as
Vidalia), thickly sliced
4 red peppers
4 yellow peppers
2 tablespoons balsamic vinegar

Red and yellow pepper sauces give this salad a bright look.

Barbecuing vegetables lends them a mellow taste. But watch them carefully and make sure they do not char.

Marinate chicken breasts in olive oil, tarragon, salt and pepper for 30 minutes. Grill over hot coals for 4 minutes on each side or until no longer pink in the center. Cool slightly and slice diagonally. Set aside.

Brush asparagus, zucchini, yellow squash, potatoes, eggplant and onion with olive oil marinade and grill over medium-hot coals until tender. Sprinkle with salt and pepper.

Grill red and yellow peppers over medium-hot coals until charred. Place in a plastic bag for 10 minutes. Remove skin and seeds. Puree red and yellow peppers separately in a food processor or blender. Stir 1 tablespoon balsamic vinegar into each puree and season with salt and pepper.

To assemble salad, cover one side of each of 4 individual dishes with a few tablespoons of red pepper puree and the other side with yellow pepper puree. Fan out slices of chicken in one corner and arrange ¼ of the vegetables in the center.

GRILLED DUCK WITH WINTER VEGETABLES

SERVES 6

INGREDIENTS

1 head radicchio
1 small curly endive
2 heads Belgian endive
2 cups (120 g) fresh
spinach leaves
1 fennel bulb, sliced
¼ cup (60 mL) walnut oil
2 tablespoons champagne
vinegar
salt and pepper to taste
2 ripe pears, peeled, sliced
1 tablespoon fresh lemon juice
2 cups (230 g) fresh cranberries
½ cup (115 g) granulated sugar
¼ cup (60 mL) soy sauce
2 tablespoons sesame oil
2 tablespoons minced
fresh ginger
1 tablespoon chopped garlic
4 boneless, skinless duck
breast halves
¼ cup (30 g) chopped walnuts

Oriental marinated duck breasts served with sliced fennel, pear and cranberry dressing will brighten any wintertime menu.

Arrange radicchio leaves on a platter. Tear both endives and spinach into bite-size pieces. In a bowl combine greens and fennel. Combine walnut oil, champagne vinegar, salt and pepper; pour over greens and toss lightly. Arrange over radicchio. Toss pear with lemon juice.

Cook cranberries and sugar for 10 minutes or until cranberries pop. Crush with a fork. Remove and cool.

Combine soy sauce, sesame oil, ginger and garlic. Marinate duck breasts in this mixture for 30 minutes. Remove and grill 4 minutes on each side or until just pink inside. Slice diagonally.

Arrange duck slices in the center of the greens and fan pear slices around edge. Sprinkle with walnuts and serve with cranberry sauce.

Opposite: Grilled Duck with Winter Vegetables

Tacos have become mainstream American fare. Serve with mugs of beer and play some mariachi music on the stereo.

Combine olive oil, vinegar, chili powder, garlic, oregano, cumin, salt, pepper, and red pepper flakes in a bottle and shake until well blended. Marinate steak in ½ cup (120 mL) of mixture for several hours in refrigerator. Grill steak over hot coals for 8 to 10 minutes on each side or to desired doneness. Slice thinly across the grain.

Arrange lettuce on serving platter; top with tortilla chips and kidney beans.

Brush avocado slices with lime juice. Arrange steak, avocado, eggs, and tomatoes on top. Drizzle with remaining salad dressing. Sprinkle with cheddar cheese and garnish with olives, dollops of sour cream and chopped cilantro.

TACO SALAD

SERVES 6

INGREDIENTS

½ cup (120 mL) olive oil
¼ cup (60 mL) red wine vinegar
1 teaspoon chili powder
1 clove garlic, pressed
¼ teaspoon dried oregano
⅛ teaspoon ground cumin
salt and pepper to taste
¼ teaspoon red pepper flakes
1½ pounds (675 g) boneless
sirloin steak
1 small head iceberg lettuce
2 to 3 cups (120 to 180 g)
tortilla chips
2 cups (450 g) cooked
kidney beans
1 ripe avocado, sliced
2 tablespoons fresh lime juice
3 hard-cooked eggs, sliced
2 ripe tomatoes, cut into wedges
1 cup (115 g) shredded
cheddar cheese
½ cup (60 g) California
black olives
sour cream
chopped cilantro

CHINESE NOODLES WITH SHRIMP AND VEGETABLES

SERVES 4

INGREDIENTS

¾ pound (350 g) Chinese
creamy-style noodles
(found in Oriental markets)
or linguine, cooked
according to package
directions, drained
2 tablespoons sesame oil
1 pound (450 g) large
shrimp, shelled
2 tablespoons peanut oil
2 tablespoons minced
fresh ginger
1 tablespoon minced fresh garlic
2 cups (230 g) broccoli
flowerettes
2 sweet potatoes, peeled,
julienned
7-ounce (200-g) can water
chestnuts, halved
¼ cup (60 mL) soy sauce
¼ cup (60 mL) dry sherry
2 tablespoons rice vinegar
4 scallions, chopped

Oriental cuisine doesn't include many salads but this one is a complete meal.

Rinse noodles in cold water and drain. Toss with sesame oil. Set aside.

Cook shrimp for 3 minutes in lightly salted boiling water. Drain and set aside.

In a wok or large skillet heat oil and stir-fry ginger and garlic for 1 minute. Add broccoli and cook 2 minutes. Add sweet potatoes and cook 2 minutes longer. Add water chestnuts and shrimp and heat through.

Combine soy sauce, sherry and rice vinegar. Add to vegetables and stir until well combined.

Place cold noodles in a shallow serving dish. Spoon vegetable mixture on top and sprinkle with scallions.

PASTA SALAD

Pasta salads have become more sophisticated than the elbow macaroni salads we remember. They get better if flavors are allowed to meld for a few hours. Never overcook the pasta. Cook them like the Italians do—to the point where they offer the slightest resistance to the bite.

ORZO AND CRAB SALAD

SERVES 4

INGREDIENTS

1 cup (200 g) orzo
½ cup (60 g) diced red pepper
4 scallions, chopped
2 stalks celery, chopped
1 pound (450 g) crabmeat
or imitation crab,
coarsely chopped
⅔ cup (160 mL) mayonnaise
¼ cup (60 mL) white wine
1 tablespoon fresh lemon juice
1 teaspoon Worcestershire sauce
salt and pepper to taste
½ pound (225 g) snow peas,
stems removed
12 cherry tomatoes, halved

Orzo is a tiny rice-shaped pasta that is equally at home in soup or a salad.

Cook orzo according to package directions. Drain in a colander and rinse under cold water until cool. Combine with red pepper, scallions, celery and crab.

Mix together mayonnaise, white wine, lemon juice, Worcestershire, salt and pepper.

Blanch snow peas for 30 seconds in a large quantity of boiling water. Drain and rinse under cold water. Pat dry with paper towel.

To serve, arrange snow peas facing outward around edge of a serving platter. Pile crabmeat mixture in center and ring tomatoes, cut side down, between the crabmeat and the snow peas.

Smoked salmon dresses up humble pasta. Good with sliced grilled steak.

Cook shells according to package directions. Rinse in cold water and drain well. Toss with 2 tablespoons olive oil. Cut the salmon into bite-size pieces. Cook peas until tender.

Combine ¾ cup olive oil, lemon juice and cream and whisk until blended. Add salt and pepper to taste. In a serving bowl combine pasta, salmon and peas. Pour dressing over and toss lightly. Sprinkle with capers.

SMOKED SALMON AND PASTA SALAD

SERVES 4

INGREDIENTS

½ pound (225 g) small
pasta shells
2 tablespoons olive oil
6 ounces (200 g) smoked salmon
1 cup (115 g) green peas
¾ cup (180 mL) olive oil
juice of 1 lemon
2 tablespoons heavy cream
salt and pepper to taste
2 tablespoons small capers,
rinsed

PASTA PRIMAVERA

SERVES 8

INGREDIENTS

¾ pound (350 g) pasta
2 tablespoons olive oil
2 ripe tomatoes, peeled, seeded,
cut into strips
1 red pepper, roasted, seeded,
peeled, cut into strips
2 cups (230 g) broccoli
flowerettes, blanched
2 minutes
2 small zucchini, sliced,
blanched 1 minute
2 tablespoons chopped
black olives
⅔ cup (160 mL) olive oil
3 tablespoons red wine vinegar
¼ cup (30 g) chopped
Italian parsley
¼ cup (30 g) chopped
fresh basil
salt and pepper to taste

No broccoli? Substitute cauliflower. No zucchini? Substitute yellow summer squash. Add or subtract at will—peas, carrots, asparagus.

Cook pasta according to package directions. Rinse in cold water and drain well. Toss with 2 tablespoons olive oil and set aside. In a large bowl combine tomato, red pepper, broccoli, zucchini and olives. Add pasta and toss gently.

Combine ⅔ cup olive oil, vinegar, parsley, basil, salt and pepper in a food processor or blender and blend until smooth. Pour over pasta and toss.

A no-cook sauce based on goat cheese and pepperoni is whipped up in a blender while the tortellini are cooking. What could be easier?

Cook tortellini according to package directions. Drain and toss with 2 tablespoons olive oil.

In food processor puree goat cheese, olive oil, pepperoni, vinegar, garlic, salt and pepper.

Combine the tortellini, dressing, chopped tomatoes and basil. Toss lightly and serve at room temperature.

TORTELLINI WITH CREAMY PEPPERONI DRESSING

SERVES 4

INGREDIENTS

¾ pound (350 g) tortellini
2 tablespoons olive oil
¼ pound (115 g) goat cheese
½ cup (120 mL) olive oil
2 ounces (60 g) pepperoni,
cut into small chunks
2 tablespoons red wine vinegar
1 clove garlic
salt and pepper to taste
2 plum tomatoes, peeled,
seeded, chopped
8 leaves fresh basil, cut into
¼-inch (.5-cm) strips

CHICKEN PASTA SALAD WITH THREE PEPPERS

SERVES 6

INGREDIENTS

1 pound (450 g) fusilli or
rotelle pasta
¼ cup (60 mL) olive oil
1 pound (450 g) chicken breasts,
cut into 1-inch pieces
2 cups (500 mL) chicken stock
2 tablespoons olive oil
2 cloves garlic, minced
1 yellow pepper, thinly sliced
1 red pepper, thinly sliced
1 green pepper, thinly sliced
1 cup sliced black olives
4-ounce (115-g) can green chili
peppers, chopped
½ cup (120 mL) light olive oil
¼ cup (60 mL) fresh lime juice
¼ cup (30 g) chopped cilantro
1 small tomato, cut into chunks
1 small shallot
2 cloves garlic
1 fresh jalapeño pepper, seeded
lettuce leaves
4 scallions, chopped

Looking for a pasta salad suitable for a fancy buffet? Stop right here.

Cook pasta according to package directions. Rinse in cold water and drain. Toss pasta with ¼ cup olive oil and chill.

Bring chicken pieces and stock to a simmer and poach over low heat for 10 minutes or until done. Heat 2 tablespoons olive oil and sauté minced garlic for 2 minutes over medium-high heat. Add peppers and sauté for 2 minutes. Combine with chicken, pasta, olives and chili peppers.

In blender combine ½ cup olive oil, lime juice, cilantro, tomato, shallot, garlic and jalapeño and process until smooth. Pour over salad ingredients and toss lightly. Arrange lettuce leaves on serving platter and top with chicken mixture. Sprinkle with chopped scallions.

Opposite: Chicken Pasta Salad with Three Peppers
Overleaf: Four Bean Salad (p. 30)

RICE, BEAN, GRAIN AND BREAD SALADS

Rice, beans, grains and bread are economical foods that are given stellar positions when gussied up in tasty combinations to please the most particular palates.

CHICKEN AND WILD RICE SALAD

SERVES 4

INGREDIENTS

2 cups (230 g) cooked
wild rice, cooled
2 cups (230 g) cooked
chicken, cubed
1 Granny Smith apple, chopped
½ cup (60 g) thinly
sliced celery
4 scallions, chopped
½ cup (120 mL) mayonnaise
½ cup (120 mL) sour cream
1 teaspoon chopped fresh
tarragon, or
¼ teaspoon dried
1 teaspoon Dijon mustard
2 tablespoons almond oil
leaf lettuce
¼ cup (30 g) slivered
almonds, toasted

Wild rice is a native American grain, traditionally harvested by the Chippewa Indians in the Lake Superior area. These days it is also commercially grown.

In a medium bowl combine wild rice, chicken, apple, celery and scallions.

In a separate bowl combine mayonnaise, sour cream, tarragon, mustard and almond oil. Pour over chicken mixture and toss lightly.

Arrange lettuce on 4 serving plates and top with chicken mixture. Sprinkle with almonds.

A lentil and rice salad can play a
fine supporting role with a lamb or
pork roast.

In a medium saucepan combine
lentils with 2 cups chicken stock.
Cook over medium heat for 30 to 40
minutes or until lentils are done; do
not overcook, or they will split. Let
cool.

Cook rice, covered, in 1 cup chicken
stock for 18 minutes. Rinse in cold
water and cool.

Combine lentils, rice, nuts, red
pepper and parsley in a bowl.

Whisk together olive oil, lemon juice,
vinegar, salt and pepper. Pour over
lentil mixture and toss lightly.

Line serving bowl with lettuce leaves,
cut ends down. Pile lentil mixture
into bowl and garnish with chopped
scallions.

LENTILS AND RICE
SALAD

SERVES 6

INGREDIENTS

1 cup (200 g) dried lentils
2 cups (500 mL) chicken stock
½ cup (100 g) rice
1 cup (240 mL) chicken stock
½ cup (60 g) chopped walnuts or
pecans
1 small red pepper, diced
¼ cup (30 g) chopped parsley
½ cup (120 mL) olive oil
2 tablespoons fresh lemon juice
1 tablespoon red wine vinegar
salt and pepper to taste
romaine lettuce leaves
4 scallions, chopped

INDIAN RICE SALAD

SERVES 4

INGREDIENTS

1 cup (200 g) rice, preferably basmati
2 tablespoons vegetable oil
¼ cup (30 g) chopped cashews
¼ teaspoon ground cinnamon
2 tablespoons fresh lime juice
2 tablespoons chopped mint
2 tablespoons chopped cilantro
1 cup (240 mL) cooked green peas
2 tablespoons unsweetened coconut

The unique flavor of cilantro makes this rice salad rather exotic. Serve as a side dish with roasted chicken.

Cook rice according to package directions. Rinse under cold water, drain well and toss with oil.

In a separate bowl combine cashews, cinnamon, lime juice, mint, cilantro and yogurt. Mix well and pour over rice. Add peas and coconut and toss lightly.

This Middle Eastern salad is a party favorite and is especially good with lamb.

Rinse bulgur under cold water. Combine with boiling water and let stand for 1 hour. Place in a strainer and press out any remaining liquid.

Transfer to medium bowl and add parsley, scallions and mint. Toss lightly.

Combine olive oil, lemon juice, salt and pepper and whisk with a fork. Add to bulgur and toss lightly. Mound on romaine leaves and garnish around the edges with tomato halves and olives. Set sprig of parsley on top.

TABBOULI SALAD

SERVES 6

INGREDIENTS

1½ cups (275 g) cracked
wheat (bulgur)
2½ cups (600 mL) boiling water
½ cup (60 g) minced Italian
parsley
½ cup (60 g) chopped scallions
¼ cup (30 g) chopped mint
leaves
½ cup (120 mL) olive oil
¼ cup (60 mL) fresh
lemon juice
salt and pepper to taste
romaine lettuce
12 cherry tomatoes, halved
½ cup (60 g) olives,
preferably Gaeta
parsley sprig

FOUR BEAN SALAD

SERVES 12

INGREDIENTS

1-pound (450-g) can red
kidney beans
1-pound (450-g) can chick peas
1-pound (450-g) can black beans
1-pound (450-g) can pinto beans
¼ cup (30 g) chopped pimiento
¼ cup (30 g) chopped
green pepper
¼ cup (30 g) chopped red onion
2 cloves garlic, minced
2 tablespoons chopped
Italian parsley
½ cup (120 mL) olive oil
2 tablespoons fresh lemon juice
½ teaspoon dried oregano
salt and pepper to taste

Bean lovers will really go for this medley. Serve as part of a buffet or with beef or chicken dishes.

Drain beans in strainer and rinse under cold water. Drain again. Place in a bowl with pimiento, green pepper, onion, garlic and parsley. Whisk together olive oil, lemon juice, oregano, salt and pepper; pour over beans. Toss lightly. Chill.

The humble black bean gets a splash of color from crunchy red peppers and tomatoes and, since the combo travels well, is good for picnics at the beach.

Drain beans in strainer and rinse under cold water. Drain again. Place in a bowl with red pepper, scallions, tomatoes, celery and garlic. Add olive oil, lime juice, salt and pepper and toss lightly. Serve on lettuce leaves.

BLACK BEAN SALAD

SERVES 6

INGREDIENTS

2 1-pound (450-g) cans
black beans
1 red pepper, seeded, diced
6 scallions, chopped
2 tomatoes, peeled, seeded,
chopped
2 stalks celery, diced
3 cloves garlic, finely chopped
¼ cup (60 mL) olive oil
juice of 1 lime
salt and pepper to taste
lettuce leaves

ITALIAN BREAD SALAD

SERVES 8

INGREDIENTS

1 pound (450 g) Tuscan-style
bread, three to four days old
3 cups (750 mL) cold water
1 large red onion
1½ pounds ripe tomatoes
3 stalks celery
1 cucumber, peeled, seeded
12 fresh basil leaves, torn
2 tablespoons capers, rinsed
1 cup (240 mL) olive oil
¼ cup (60 mL) balsamic vinegar
salt and pepper to taste
arugula leaves

Tuscan bread has a hard crust and a dense, chewy interior. If it is unavailable, substitute Italian or French bread.

Place bread in a bowl and cover with cold water. Soak bread for 1 hour. Remove and squeeze out as much water as possible. Pull bread apart into ½-inch (1-cm) pieces.

While bread is soaking, prepare vegetables. Coarsely chop onion. Remove skins from tomatoes, seed and coarsely chop. Slice celery and cucumber.

Combine the bread, onion, tomatoes, celery, cucumber, basil and capers. Cover and refrigerate 2 hours. Combine the olive oil, vinegar, salt and pepper. Pour over bread mixture and serve on arugula leaves.

Opposite: Crudité Salad (p. 38)
Overleaf: Corn-off-the-Cob Salad (p. 36)

VEGETABLE SALADS

What better way to eat vegetables than in a colorful medley of tastes and textures. They also make a good alternative to green salads because they can be prepared in advance.

POTATO-TOMATO SALAD

SERVES 6

INGREDIENTS

2 pounds (900 g) small
new potatoes
1 cucumber, peeled, cut into
¼-inch (.5-cm) slices
1 green pepper, diced
3 stalks celery, thinly sliced
4 scallions, sliced
⅓ cup (80 mL) mayonnaise
⅓ cup (80 mL) sour cream
1 tablespoon chopped
fresh tarragon,
or ½ teaspoon dried
salt and pepper to taste
2 ripe tomatoes, cut into chunks
lettuce leaves

Forget plain ol' potato salad. This version includes rosy tomato chunks, cucumber, green pepper, celery and scallions for added color and flavor. Good with grilled meats.

Place potatoes in large saucepan and cover with water. Cook for 20 minutes or until tender; drain. When cool enough to handle, cut into quarters.

In a large bowl combine potatoes, cucumber, green pepper, celery and scallions.

In a separate bowl blend mayonnaise, sour cream, tarragon, salt and pepper. Pour over vegetables and stir gently to combine. Refrigerate for about 1 hour. Just before serving, gently stir in tomatoes. Serve over lettuce.

*When your garden explodes with
tomatoes, zucchini and peppers and
you don't want to cook, it's time to
make ratatouille salad.*

*In a bowl combine tomatoes,
zucchini, yellow squash, green and
red peppers, mushrooms, onion,
olives and capers.*

*In a blender or food processor
combine olive oil, vinegar, parsley,
garlic, salt and pepper and blend
until smooth. Pour over vegetables
and toss gently.*

RATATOUILLE SALAD

SERVES 6

INGREDIENTS

2 cups (450 g) peeled, seeded,
chopped plum tomatoes
2 small zucchini, diced
2 small yellow crookneck
squash, diced
1 green pepper, diced
1 red pepper, diced
2 cups (230 g) sliced mushrooms
1 small red onion, diced
¼ cup (30 g) sliced black olives
2 tablespoons capers, rinsed
⅔ cup (160 mL) olive oil
3 tablespoons balsamic vinegar
2 tablespoons chopped
Italian parsley
2 cloves garlic, chopped
salt and pepper to taste

CORN-OFF-THE-COB SALAD

SERVES 4

INGREDIENTS

4 ears fresh corn
1 red pepper, diced
3 scallions, chopped
1 tablespoon chopped
fresh tarragon
¼ cup (60 mL) vegetable oil
2 tablespoons cider vinegar
salt and pepper to taste
Bibb lettuce
4 slices bacon, cooked and
crumbled

Fresh corn doesn't always have to be eaten on the cob.

Cut kernels from corn cobs and blanch 1 minute in boiling water. Drain well. Combine with red pepper, scallion and tarragon.

Whisk together oil, vinegar, salt and pepper. Pour over vegetables and toss lightly. Arrange on lettuce leaves and sprinkle with bacon.

When the price of lettuce goes sky-high during the winter months, rely on seasonal vegetables for the salad course.

Remove tops of fennel bulbs and discard; cut fennel into wedges. Cook beets in boiling water until tender, about 15 minutes. Rinse in cold water and slip off skins. Cut beets into wedges. Separate endive into leaves and arrange on individual serving plates; top with fennel and beets.

Combine lemon juice, walnut oil, salt and pepper. Pour dressing over vegetables; sprinkle with Gorgonzola and nuts.

FENNEL AND BEET SALAD WITH GORGONZOLA DRESSING

SERVES 4

INGREDIENTS

2 fennel bulbs
1 pound (450 g) small beets
2 Belgian endives
2 tablespoons fresh lemon juice
½ cup (120 mL) walnut oil
salt and pepper to taste
½ cup (60 g) crumbled
Gorgonzola cheese
2 tablespoons chopped
toasted walnuts

CRUDITÉ SALAD

SERVES 6

INGREDIENTS

½ cup (120 mL) olive oil
3 tablespoons red wine vinegar
1 teaspoon Dijon mustard
2 tablespoons finely chopped
Italian parsley
salt and pepper to taste
½ pound (225 g) tender young
green beans
3 medium carrots, peeled,
cut into thin strips
2 red peppers, seeded,
cut into thin strips
lettuce leaves
2 scallions, chopped

Crudités are meant to be served with dips, but here the raw vegetables are tossed with a classic vinaigrette dressing.

For dressing, whisk together oil, vinegar, mustard, parsley, salt and pepper; set aside.

Cook beans in boiling water for about 10 minutes or until tender. Rinse in cold water, drain and pat dry. Combine in bowl with ¼ cup (60 mL) dressing and marinate 15 minutes.

Blanch carrots in boiling water for 2 minutes. Rinse in cold water, drain and pat dry. Combine in bowl with ¼ cup (60 mL) dressing and marinate 15 minutes.

Marinate red pepper in remaining dressing 15 minutes. Arrange vegetables on lettuce leaves and sprinkle with scallions.

Toss a crunchy assortment of colorful vegetables with an Oriental-inspired dressing and garnish it with nutty toasted sesame seeds. What more could you want to accompany grilled fish?

Remove strings from snow peas and blanch pods in boiling water for 1 minute. Rinse under cold water and set aside. Blanch cauliflower and broccoli in boiling water for 3 minutes. Rinse under cold water and set aside. Combine snow peas, cauliflower, broccoli, water chestnuts, bamboo shoots and red pepper in a bowl.

Beat together vegetable oil, sesame oil, rice vinegar, garlic, sugar, sesame seeds, salt and pepper. Pour over vegetables and toss lightly. Sprinkle with chopped scallions.

ORIENTAL-STYLE VEGETABLE SALAD

SERVES 6

INGREDIENTS

4 ounces (115 g) snow peas
2 cups (230 g) cauliflower flowerettes
2 cups (230 g) broccoli flowerettes
7-ounce (200-g) can water chestnuts, sliced
7-ounce (200-g) can bamboo shoots, sliced
1 red pepper, thinly sliced
½ cup (120 mL) vegetable oil
2 tablespoons sesame oil
2 tablespoons rice vinegar
2 cloves garlic, minced
1 teaspoon granulated sugar
2 tablespoons toasted sesame seeds
salt and pepper to taste
4 scallions, chopped

39

GADO-GADO

SERVES 8

INGREDIENTS

1 pound (450 g) fresh spinach
½ pound (225 g) green beans
1 cup (115 g) shredded cabbage
4 medium-size new potatoes
2 cups (225 g) bean sprouts
2 cucumbers, peeled and sliced
2 hard-cooked eggs, coarsely
chopped
2 tablespoons vegetable oil
1 small onion, chopped
2 cloves garlic, finely chopped
½ teaspoon anchovy paste
½ cup (125 g) chunk-style
peanut butter
1 tablespoon brown sugar
1 tablespoon grated fresh ginger
1 tablespoon grated lemon peel
1 small fresh red or green chili
pepper, finely chopped
1 cup (240 mL) unsweetened
coconut milk (available in
Oriental and Latin
American markets)

Gado-Gado (one of the most famous Indonesian salads) combines sweet, sour and spicy flavors. It is often served with riijsttafel or "rice table."

Trim spinach, wash and pat dry. Trim green beans, cook until tender, rinse in cold water and cut into 2-inch (5-cm) lengths. Blanch cabbage 2 minutes in boiling water; rinse in cold water. Cook potatoes for 20 minutes or until tender. Cool and cut into wedges.

Arrange spinach on a serving platter. Arrange the green beans, cabbage, potato, sprouts and cucumber in a circle on the spinach. Sprinkle with chopped egg and serve with dressing.

To make dressing, heat oil over medium heat and sauté onion and garlic 3 minutes. Stir in anchovy paste, peanut butter, brown sugar, ginger, lemon peel, chili and coconut milk. Cook over low heat for a few minutes until smooth, stirring constantly. Let cool before serving.

Opposite: Gado-Gado
Overleaf: Citrus Salad with Ginger Yogurt
Dressing (p. 45)

FRUIT SALADS

Not all salads are green and leafy and not all fruit is eaten as dessert. We have choices—a first course, a side dish or a whole meal. Each puts a sunny mood into any menu.

BLUEBERRY SALAD

SERVES 4

INGREDIENTS

1 Golden Delicious apple
1 Bartlett pear
1 navel orange
1 cup (115 g) fresh blueberries
4 Boston lettuce leaves
¼ cup (60 mL) mild
vegetable oil
2 tablespoons raspberry vinegar
pinch of salt
4 sprigs mint

The flavors of crunchy apple, buttery pear, juicy orange and luscious blueberries are melded together with a raspberry vinegar dressing.

Core apple and pear; cut into thin wedges. Peel orange and slice crosswise. Pick over blueberries, removing any that are soft.

Arrange lettuce leaves on 4 plates. Divide fruit among plates. Combine oil, vinegar and salt and pour over fruit. Garnish with mint.

No need to give up fruit salad just because the wind is blowing snow around. Here's one, not too sweet, that can be served as a first course for a winter dinner party.

Combine pears, bananas and apples in a large bowl and toss with 2 tablespoons lemon juice. Add orange segments, grapes, raisins and pecans and toss lightly. Spoon fruit into 8 individual bowls. To make dressing, mix together sour cream, orange juice concentrate and 2 teaspoons lemon juice. Top fruit with dressing and serve.

WINTER FRUIT SALAD

SERVES 8

INGREDIENTS

4 ripe pears, cored, pared
2 bananas, sliced
2 Delicious apples, cored, diced
2 tablespoons fresh lemon juice
2 navel oranges, skinned,
separated into segments
1 cup (115 g) Thompson
seedless grapes
1 cup (115 g) seedless red grapes
½ cup (100 g) golden raisins
¼ cup (30 g) chopped pecans
1 cup (240 mL) sour cream
3 tablespoons undiluted orange
juice concentrate
2 teaspoons fresh lemon juice

FRUIT SALAD WITH GINGER DRESSING

SERVES 6

INGREDIENTS

1 small cantaloupe, peeled and
cut into balls or chunks
½ large honeydew melon, peeled
and cut into balls or chunks
1 cup (115 g) strawberries,
hulled, halved
1 cup (115 g) seedless
Thompson grapes
2 peaches, sliced
2 nectarines, sliced
1 tablespoon grated fresh ginger
2 tablespoons brown sugar
1 cup (240 mL) heavy
cream, whipped
1 cup (100 g) shredded coconut
mint sprigs

Shredded coconut lends a pleasant crunch to this colorful array of summer fruit.

Combine cantaloupe, honeydew, strawberries, grapes, peaches and nectarines in a bowl. Sprinkle with ginger and brown sugar; toss lightly. Spoon into individual serving dishes, top with a dollop of whipped cream and sprinkle with coconut. Garnish with a sprig of mint.

Citrus fruit and sweet red onion are a traditional match that gets a new dimension with the addition of crystallized ginger and pecans.

Peel orange and grapefruit and cut off white pith. To section fruit, cut down to center on both sides of membrane and remove segments. Separate onion slices into rings. Arrange watercress on individual plates and top with orange, grapefruit and onion rings.

Whisk together ginger, yogurt, grape juice, vinegar and oil until well blended. Spoon over salad and garnish with pecans.

CITRUS SALAD WITH GINGER YOGURT DRESSING

SERVES 4

INGREDIENTS

2 large navel oranges
1 grapefruit
1 small sweet red onion, thinly sliced
watercress sprigs
2 tablespoons chopped crystallized ginger
¼ cup (60 mL) plain yogurt
½ cup (120 mL) white grape juice
1 tablespoon vegetable oil
chopped pecans

BERRIES AND MELON WITH HONEY DRESSING

SERVES 4

INGREDIENTS

2 cups (225 g) blueberries
2 cups (225 g) strawberries
1 cantaloupe
½ cup (120 mL) sour cream
½ cup (120 mL) plain yogurt
¼ cup (60 mL) honey
1 tablespoon grated orange peel
¼ teaspoon grated nutmeg
lettuce
4 mint sprigs

Here is the perfect summer salad when berries are at their best.

Pick over blueberries, rinse and pat dry. Rinse strawberries and pat dry; cut large ones in half. Peel and halve cantaloupe; remove seeds and slice into 16 wedges.

Combine sour cream, yogurt, honey, orange peel and nutmeg and stir well.

Line 4 plates with lettuce and arrange 4 cantaloupe wedges in a circle on each. Pile berries in the center and spoon dressing over fruit just before serving. Garnish with a sprig of mint.

GREEN SALADS

When we think of salad, we naturally think of green salads first; they are the most popular and versatile. Whether salad greens are torn by hand or cut with a knife is up to the cook, but make sure the greens are dry before adding any dressing. A salad spinner is a good investment.

MESCLUN WITH RASPBERRY DRESSING

SERVES 6

INGREDIENTS

¼ cup (60 mL) vegetable oil
2 tablespoons raspberry vinegar
1 tablespoon heavy cream
salt and pepper to taste
¼ cup (50 g) pine nuts
6 to 8 cups mesclun (mixed baby
greens) or a variety of
tender lettuces
1 bunch watercress, trimmed
½ cup (60 g) fresh raspberries

Mesclun is a combination of several baby lettuces sowed and harvested at the same time. The greens are chosen because they have different shapes and colors. The leaves are often left whole.

Whisk together oil, vinegar, cream, salt and pepper.

Toast pine nuts for 6 minutes or until golden in a preheated 350°F (175°C) oven, taking care not to burn them. Toss mesclun and watercress with dressing and arrange on individual dishes. Sprinkle with toasted pine nuts and raspberries.

Opposite: Mesclun with Raspberry Dressing

*The surprise in this otherwise
standard salad comes from the
almond oil used in the dressing and
the toasted almond garnish. Serve it
with broiled fish.*

*Wash greens, pat dry and tear into
bite-size pieces. Whisk together the
vinegar and cream until foamy. Add
oil, salt and pepper and whisk until
well blended. Just before serving, pour
dressing over greens and toss gently.
Sprinkle with almonds.*

GREENS WITH CREAMY TARRAGON DRESSING

SERVES 6

INGREDIENTS

6 cups (350 g) greens (spinach,
Bibb lettuce, romaine)
4 teaspoons white wine vinegar
⅓ cup (80 mL) heavy cream
2 tablespoons almond oil
salt and pepper to taste
2 tablespoons chopped
fresh tarragon
2 tablespoons toasted almonds

Opposite: Seafood Salad (p. 67)

GREEN SALAD WITH LEMON-CHIVE DRESSING

SERVES 6

INGREDIENTS

1 small head romaine lettuce
2 heads endive
½ pound (225 g) fresh spinach
1 bunch watercress
2 cups (230 g) sliced mushrooms
½ cup (120 mL) olive oil
3 tablespoons fresh lemon juice
salt and pepper to taste
1 teaspoon Worcestershire sauce
3 tablespoons chopped
fresh chives

Assertive spinach and watercress are paired with milder romaine and endive. Serve as a palate cleanser after a hearty pork roast.

Separate romaine and endive leaves. Trim spinach and watercress; wash and pat dry. Tear into bite-size pieces. Combine with mushrooms.

Whisk together the olive oil, lemon juice, salt, pepper and Worcestershire sauce. Just before serving, toss dressing with greens and sprinkle with chives.

Though the ingredients are familiar, the combination of colorful shapes makes a dramatic presentation.

Trim spinach; wash and pat dry. Carefully tear leaves into bite-size pieces. Place in a bowl with cauliflower and red pepper.

Whisk together olive oil, lemon juice, garlic, oregano, salt and pepper. Pour over vegetables and toss lightly.

RED, WHITE AND GREEN SALAD

SERVES 6

INGREDIENTS

1 pound (450 g) fresh spinach
2 cups (230 g) cauliflower
flowerettes
2 red peppers, cut into strips
¼ cup (60 mL) olive oil
2 tablespoons fresh lemon juice
1 clove garlic, pressed
1 teaspoon fresh oregano,
or ¼ teaspoon dried
salt and pepper to taste

GARDEN SALAD WITH FENNEL VINAIGRETTE

SERVES 4

INGREDIENTS

2 cups (230 g) thinly sliced
red cabbage
1 red pepper, sliced
2 small yellow crookneck
squash, sliced
2 small zucchini, sliced
1 small fennel bulb, sliced
2 cups (230 g) sliced mushrooms
½ cup (120 mL) olive oil
¼ cup (60 mL) red wine vinegar
1 teaspoon Dijon mustard
2 cloves garlic, minced
salt and pepper to taste
¼ teaspoon fennel
seeds, crushed
8 leaves radicchio
8 cherry tomatoes

Sliced fennel and fennel seeds add a slight licorice flavor to this lively salad with lots of colorful vegetables.

In a bowl combine red cabbage, pepper, yellow squash, zucchini, fennel and mushrooms.

Combine olive oil, vinegar, mustard, garlic, salt, pepper and fennel seeds and beat with fork to blend. Pour dressing over vegetables and toss lightly. Arrange radicchio on 4 plates and divide vegetables among them. Garnish with cherry tomatoes.

A variety of salad greens and green vegetables is accented by a mysterious "something" in the dressing. Few will identify it as anchovy.

Trim spinach and watercress; wash and pat dry. Peel and slice avocado and rub with lemon juice. Cook peas and broccoli separately until tender.

To make dressing, combine mayonnaise, sour cream, anchovies, scallions, parsley, tarragon, garlic, 1 tablespoon lemon juice, vinegar, salt and pepper in a blender or food processor and blend until smooth.

Combine vegetables in a large bowl and serve dressing on the side.

GREEN, GREEN, GREEN

SERVES 6

INGREDIENTS

1 pound (450 g) fresh spinach
1 bunch watercress
1 avocado
fresh lemon juice
1 cup (115 g) green peas
2 cups (230 g) broccoli flowerettes
1 cup (240 mL) mayonnaise, preferably homemade
½ cup (120 mL) sour cream
3 anchovy fillets, mashed
3 scallions, finely chopped
3 tablespoons chopped Italian parsley
1 tablespoon chopped fresh tarragon
1 clove garlic, finely chopped
1 tablespoon cider vinegar
salt and pepper to taste

RADDICCHIO, ARUGULA AND ENDIVE SALAD

SERVES 4

INGREDIENTS

1 head radicchio
2 bunches arugula
2 heads Belgian endive
½ cup (120 mL) olive oil
2 tablespoons red wine vinegar
1 teaspoon Dijon mustard
1 clove garlic, finely chopped
salt and pepper to taste

Delicate Belgian endive matches well with bitter radicchio and peppery arugula.

Wash radicchio, arugula and endive and pat dry. Tear into bite-size pieces. Whisk together oil, vinegar, mustard, garlic, salt and pepper. Pour over greens and toss lightly. Serve immediately.

In 1924, during the middle of
American Prohibition, Caesar
Cardini ran a restaurant in
Tijuana, Mexico. Lots of Hollywood
stars and Navy men from San Diego
would venture down to his
restaurant for a night on the town.
During a particularly busy July 4th
weekend, Cardini experienced what
every restaurateur fears—he ran out
of food. All he had left in the kitchen
were romaine lettuce, eggs, Romano
cheese, bread, olive oil and lemons.
Truly inspired, Cardini put together
what he had and created the Caesar
salad. But because he feared that
salad did not make a substantial
enough entree, he added his own
flourishes and presented the dish
tableside along with peppermills,
cheese graters and crisp croutons.

Three decades later, the International
Society of Journeymen Chefs presented
Cardini with an award calling the
Caesar salad the most original dish
to come out of North America in 50
years.

Here is his original recipe. Anchovies
were added later by other chefs; still

CAESAR SALAD

SERVES 6 TO 8

INGREDIENTS

2 medium heads chilled
romaine lettuce
juice of 1 lemon
½ teaspoon salt
½ teaspoon freshly ground black
pepper
2 eggs, coddled 1 minute
½ cup (120 mL) garlic-flavored
olive oil (see Note)
6 drops Worcestershire sauce
¼ cup (30 g) grated
Romano cheese
½ cup (30 g) warm croutons

others substituted Parmesan for Romano cheese.

Break the romaine into 2-inch pieces. Place in a large salad bowl and sprinkle the leaves with a few drops of lemon juice. Add salt and pepper.

In another bowl beat the coddled eggs and gradually add the olive oil, beating until the oil is incorporated. Beat in the Worcestershire sauce and the rest of the lemon juice.

Pour dressing over the greens, add cheese and toss 6 or 7 times, mixing thoroughly but being careful not to bruise the leaves. Add the croutons and toss 2 more times. Serve immediately.

Note

To make garlic-flavored oil, steep several slightly mashed garlic cloves in olive oil for at least 24 hours.

Opposite: Raddicchio, Arugula and Endive Salad (p. 54)
Overleaf: Cobb Salad (p. 59)

CHEESE SALADS

Europeans frequently serve cheese along with the salad course, but in this case cheese becomes part of the salad in some familiar and some not-so-familiar combinations.

GREEK SALAD

SERVES 6

INGREDIENTS

1 large head romaine lettuce
1 small red onion, cut into rings
1 green pepper, sliced
2 ripe tomatoes, cut into eighths
1 cucumber, thinly sliced
6 radishes, thinly sliced
3 scallions, sliced
6 anchovies, coarsely chopped
½ cup (115 g) black olives,
preferably Kalamata
3 tablespoons fresh lemon juice
6 tablespoons fresh olive oil
salt and pepper to taste
1 sprig mint, chopped
½ teaspoon dried oregano
4 ounces (120 g) feta cheese,
crumbled

Wash lettuce, dry and tear into small pieces. Place in a large, shallow salad bowl. Layer on top onion, green pepper, tomato, cucumber, radish, scallions, anchovies and olives.

In a small bowl whisk together lemon juice, olive oil, salt, pepper, mint and oregano. Just before serving, crumble feta on top and pour dressing over salad.

Note

Kalamata olives are black-purple in color and almond-shaped. They are imported from Greece.

Arrange lettuce on a very large platter. Top with turkey, bacon, eggs, tomatoes, scallions, avocado, watercress and cheddar cheese.

In a separate bowl combine oil, vinegar, Worcestershire sauce, garlic, mustard, salt, pepper and Roquefort cheese. Stir to combine. Pour dressing over salad and serve immediately.

COBB SALAD
FROM LOS ANGELES' BROWN DERBY RESTAURANT

SERVES 6

INGREDIENTS

1 head iceberg lettuce, shredded
2 cups (230 g) turkey in
½-in (2-cm) dice
8 slices bacon, cooked, crumbled
3 hard-cooked eggs,
finely chopped
2 tomatoes, peeled, seeded,
finely diced
4 scallions, chopped
1 avocado, peeled, diced
1 bunch watercress, trimmed,
chopped
1 cup (115 g) shredded
cheddar cheese
⅔ cup (160 mL) vegetable oil
⅓ cup (80 mL) red
wine vinegar
2 tablespoons Worcestershire
sauce
2 cloves garlic, minced
1 teaspoon Dijon mustard
salt and pepper to taste
½ cup (60 g) crumbled
Roquefort cheese

KIELBASA AND SMOKED MOZZARELLA SALAD

SERVES 4

INGREDIENTS

2 pounds (900 g) kielbasa
sausage
6 ounces (200 g) smoked
mozzarella, cut into
¼-inch (.5-cm) dice
1 red pepper, diced
1 small red onion, sliced
¼ cup (15 g) chopped parsley
2 tablespoons chopped
cornichons
½ cup (120 mL) olive oil
2 tablespoons balsamic vinegar
1 clove garlic, minced
¼ teaspoon Dijon mustard
salt and pepper to taste

Serve this hearty salad with cole slaw, steins of beer and good pumpernickel bread.

Simmer kielbasa in water to cover for 10 minutes. Drain and cool to room temperature. Cut into ½-inch (1-cm) slices. Combine with mozzarella, red pepper, red onion, parsley and cornichons.

Whisk together olive oil, balsamic vinegar, garlic, mustard, salt and pepper. Pour over kielbasa mixture and toss.

This salad is similar to one served in Provence, but we don't have to rely on the French for goat cheese any longer. It is now produced in California, upstate New York and Wisconsin.

Lightly dip goat cheese into ½ cup olive oil. Roll in breadcrumbs and refrigerate for 20 minutes. Place on a lightly oiled baking sheet and bake in a preheated 400°F (200°C) oven for 7 to 10 minutes or until golden.

In a blender or food processor combine ½ cup olive oil, lemon juice, tomato, mint, salt and pepper and blend until smooth. Wash mâche, radicchio and arugula and pat dry. Arrange on 6 individual salad plates. Top each with 2 slices warm goat cheese and a few tablespoons dressing. Serve immediately.

BAKED GOAT CHEESE WITH TOMATO-MINT DRESSING

SERVES 4 TO 6

INGREDIENTS

12-ounce (350-g) log goat cheese, cut into 1/2-inch (1-cm) rounds
½ cup (120 mL) olive oil
½ cup (60 g) dry bread crumbs
½ cup (120 mL) olive oil
2 tablespoons fresh lemon juice
1 cup peeled, seeded, chopped tomato
1 tablespoon chopped mint
salt and pepper to taste
1 head of mâche or lamb's lettuce
1 small head radicchio
2 bunches arugula

SEVEN-LAYER SALAD

SERVES 6

INGREDIENTS

2 cups (225 g) fresh green peas
1 head iceberg lettuce
¼ cup (30 g) chopped scallions
2 tablespoons chopped
green pepper
¾ cup (180 mL) mayonnaise
2 tablespoons granulated sugar
1 cup (115 g) shredded
cheddar cheese
8 slices lean bacon, cooked,
drained, crumbled

Going to a bring-a-dish supper? This is the perfect salad to take along.

Steam peas in a small amount of water until tender, about 3 minutes. Remove core from lettuce; wash leaves and pat dry. With a sharp knife, shred into ¼-inch (.5-cm) strips.

In a glass bowl layer the ingredients in this order: lettuce, peas, scallions, green pepper. Spread top with mayonnaise and sprinkle with sugar, cheddar cheese and bacon. Cover tightly with plastic wrap and refrigerate at least 8 hours.

SEAFOOD SALADS

Are there fish salads beyond tuna and shrimp? You bet. Even those who say they "hate" fish can get turned on by a wide variety of preparations.

SOUTH OF THE BORDER SHRIMP SALAD

SERVES 4

INGREDIENTS

2 ripe tomatoes, cut into wedges
1 cucumber, sliced
1 small red onion, chopped
¾ pound (350 g) cooked
shrimp, peeled
1 jalapeño pepper,
seeded, chopped
¼ cup (30 g) chopped cilantro
½ cup (120 mL) vegetable oil
3 tablespoons fresh lime juice
½ teaspoon chili powder
salt and pepper to taste
4 cups torn lettuce leaves

Jalapeño pepper and chili powder add a hot touch to this shrimp salad, but the cucumber cools things off.

In a medium bowl combine tomatoes, cucumber, onion, shrimp, jalapeño and cilantro. Toss lightly to combine.

In a small bowl whisk together oil, lime juice, chili powder, salt and pepper. Pour over salad ingredients and toss lightly. Cover and chill 1 hour. Arrange lettuce on 4 salad plates and top with shrimp mixture.

Opposite: South of the Border Shrimp Salad

Serve as a first course for a fancy sit-down dinner or for lunch on the patio.

Pat scallops dry; if large, cut in half. Heat vegetable oil in a skillet and sear scallops on both sides until just opaque.

Toss salad greens with olive oil, salt and pepper. Arrange greens in center of 4 serving plates. Arrange 6 asparagus on each plate with tips pointing out from center like spokes of wheel. Arrange the warm scallops between the asparagus.

Combine yogurt, mayonnaise, lime juice and dill and stir well. Place spoonfuls of dressing between the asparagus tips.

SEARED SCALLOPS WITH ASPARAGUS AND LIME-DILL DRESSING

SERVES 4

INGREDIENTS

1 pound (450 g) sea scallops
1 tablespoon vegetable oil
2 cups (115 g) torn salad greens
1 tablespoon olive oil
salt and pepper to taste
24 asparagus spears, trimmed, steamed until crisp tender
½ cup (120 mL) plain yogurt
½ cup (120 mL) mayonnaise
1 tablespoon fresh lime juice
2 tablespoons chopped fresh dill

Opposite: Pasta Primavera (p. 22)

MICROWAVE POACHED SALMON WITH SPINACH SALAD

SERVES 4

INGREDIENTS

4 salmon steaks, 6 ounces
(200 g) each
¼ cup (60 mL) dry white wine
2 tablespoons butter, softened
2 tablespoons chopped onion
½ teaspoon dried oregano
½ pound (225 g) large
spinach leaves
1 bunch watercress
¼ cup (60 mL) fresh
lemon juice
1 teaspoon Dijon mustard
1 egg yolk
¼ cup (30 g) fresh
tarragon leaves
1 clove garlic, pressed
salt and pepper to taste
¾ cup (180 mL) olive oil
¼ cup (30 g) toasted pine nuts

This entree works as well with tuna steaks.

Arrange salmon steaks in a glass pie plate with the thickest portions toward the outside. Pour wine over fish and cover with vented plastic wrap. Microwave on medium for 4 minutes. Remove wrap. Combine butter, onion and oregano and spread over fish. Cover with vented plastic wrap and microwave for 5 minutes on medium. Let stand at room temperature for 5 minutes, then chill.

Wash spinach and watercress and remove stems. Arrange on serving platter and arrange salmon on top.

In a food processor or blender combine lemon juice, mustard, egg yolk, tarragon, garlic, salt and pepper and blend until tarragon is pureed. With machine running, add olive oil a drop at a time until mixture begins to thicken, then add remaining oil in a steady stream and process until thickened to mayonnaise consistency. Spoon dressing over salmon and garnish with toasted pine nuts.

Serve on buffet table or as a first course.

Steam mussels in wine for about 5 minutes or until they open; discard any that do not open. Let cool slightly, then discard shells.

Place shrimp in nonaluminum saucepan with lemon juice and cover with water. Simmer just until pink. Rinse in cool water and remove shells.

Place squid in nonaluminum saucepan with vinegar and cover with water. Simmer for 2 minutes or until tender. Rinse in cool water and combine with the mussels and shrimp, red pepper and celery.

Whisk together olive oil, lemon juice, garlic, oregano, salt and pepper with fork. Pour over shellfish and toss lightly. Serve salad on a platter lined with lettuce leaves.

SEAFOOD SALAD

SERVES 6

INGREDIENTS

4 dozen mussels
1 cup (240 mL) dry white wine
1 pound (450 g) small shrimp
2 tablespoons fresh lemon juice
1 pound (450 g) cleaned squid,
cut into 1-inch (2.5-cm) pieces
2 tablespoons white
distilled vinegar
½ cup (60 g) chopped
red pepper
½ cup (60 g) diced celery
⅓ cup (80 mL) olive oil
⅓ cup (80 mL) fresh lemon juice
2 cloves garlic, finely chopped
pinch of dried oregano
salt and pepper to taste
red leaf lettuce

MUSSEL SALAD WITH APPLES AND POTATOES

SERVES 6

INGREDIENTS

48 mussels, debearded, scrubbed
1 cup (240 mL) clam juice
2 stalks celery, sliced
1 shallot, chopped
2 cloves garlic, chopped
2 tablespoons chopped Italian
parsley
3 tablespoons fresh lime juice
3 tablespoons olive oil
½ cup (120 mL) heavy cream
salt and pepper to taste
1 green apple, cored, diced
1 bunch scallions (white part
and 1 inch of green), chopped
1 cup fresh or frozen peas,
blanched one minute
1 carrot, shredded
2 russet potatoes, peeled, diced,
cooked
spinach leaves
dill sprigs

Unless you know of a beach where you can gather mussels at low tide, buy those that are being farmed commercially. They are inexpensive and do not need much scrubbing.

Combine mussels, clam juice, celery, shallot, garlic and parsley in large pot and bring to boil. Lower heat, cover and steam 5 minutes or until mussels open; discard any that do not open. Remove mussels from pot, reserving cooking liquid. When mussels cool, remove from shell and set aside.

Pour reserved liquid through strainer and discard vegetables. Boil liquid until reduced to ¼ cup (60 mL). Whisk in lime juice, olive oil, cream, salt and pepper.

In a large bowl combine mussels, apple, scallions, peas, carrot and potatoes. Toss lightly with dressing. Line serving platter with spinach leaves and arrange salad on top. Garnish with dill sprigs.

Jicama, a root vegetable that is both crunchy and juicy as well as low in calories, is combined with zucchini and carrots in a sweet-sour dressing. Smoked chicken or turkey can be substituted for the trout.

Blanch jicama and zucchini in a large quantity of boiling water for 30 seconds. Rinse in cold water. Blanch carrots for 1 minute and rinse in cold water. Skin and bone trout; break into 1-inch (2.5-cm) pieces.

Combine vinegar, soy sauce, honey, salt and pepper in a jar. Cap and shake well.

Combine jicama, zucchini and carrots. Add dressing and toss lightly.

To serve, line a platter with lettuce leaves. Arrange the vegetables evenly in the center and ring with pieces of smoked trout. Sprinkle with sesame seeds.

SMOKED TROUT WITH JICAMA

SERVES 4

INGREDIENTS

1 pound (450 g) jicama, cut into julienne
1 pound (450 g) very small zucchini, cut into julienne
1 pound (450 g) carrots, cut into julienne
4 smoked trout
½ cup (120 mL) champagne vinegar
3 tablespoons soy sauce
3 tablespoons honey
salt and pepper to taste
leaf lettuce
toasted sesame seeds

SALAD NIÇOISE

SERVES 4

INGREDIENTS

¾ cup (180 mL) olive oil
¼ cup (60 mL) red wine vinegar
2 tablespoons chopped parsley
salt and pepper to taste
6 small new potatoes,
cooked, quartered
¼ pound (115 g) whole green
beans, cooked
crisp salad greens
2 tomatoes, cut into wedges
3 hard-cooked eggs,
cut into wedges
7-ounce (200-g) can tuna,
drained
1 red onion, cut into rings
1 cup Gaeta olives
2 tablespoons capers, rinsed
6 anchovy fillets

Combine olive oil, vinegar, parsley, salt and pepper. Toss 2 tablespoons dressing over potatoes and green beans. Marinate 30 minutes.

Arrange salad greens on a serving platter; arrange potatoes and beans in center. Place tomato and egg wedges on one side, tuna and onion rings on the other. Arrange olives, capers and anchovies on top. Serve with dressing on the side.

VINEGARS

The choice of vinegar can change the character of the salad—some are strong, some are especially flavorful, others are mellow and smooth . Here are also a few recipes to make your own.

KINDS OF VINEGAR

The choice of vinegar can change the whole character of a salad. Because it is used so sparingly, buy the best you can afford. Here is a sampling of some of the vinegars available:

Apple cider vinegar was a favorite with American pioneers, who used it to make vinegar pie during fruitless winter months. Since it is made from apples, cider vinegar should smell faintly like the fruit.

Balsamic vinegar, made in Modena, Italy, is dark brown in color and has a sweet-sour flavor. Aged in oak barrels for a minimum of three years, it can be 300 years old. The cost is high, but a little goes a long way.

Champagne vinegar is imported from the Champagne region of France; it is made not from Champagne but from white wine. The vinegar is mild-tasting and good with chicken, fruit and tossed salad greens.

Fruit vinegars (blueberry, cranberry, kiwi, raspberry, strawberry) are commercially produced by steeping fresh fruit in cider vinegar. Best used in fruit and poultry salads.

Herb vinegars (e.g., basil, tarragon, sage) are made by steeping fresh herbs in heated vinegar. Good for green salads, potato salads and mayonnaise.

Rice vinegar is low in acidity and slightly sweet. Use on vegetable, seafood and Oriental salads.

Malt vinegar, made from barley, is beer-colored and is traditionally used on fish and chips. Use it on meat and potato salads.

Red and white wine vinegars are the most popular types for vinaigrette dressings. Good for just about any salads. Buy in small quantities and discard when the vinegar turns cloudy.

Sherry vinegar, imported from Spain, has a mellow flavor. Good with fish, meat, poultry and salads.

Change the flavor of this vinegar by adjusting the selection of herbs.

Combine vinegar, herbs, garlic and peppercorns. Pour into a bottle and let stand at room temperature for about 2 weeks. Strain and discard herbs, garlic and peppercorns. Pour vinegar into a sterilized bottle. Add a fresh herb sprig, if desired.

MEDITERRANEAN VINEGAR

MAKES 2 CUPS (500 mL)

INGREDIENTS

2 cups (500 mL) red wine
vinegar
1 cup (115 g) chopped fresh
herbs (parsley, oregano,
basil, rosemary)
2 cloves garlic
6 whole peppercorns

BLUEBERRY VINEGAR

MAKES 2 CUPS (500 mL)

INGREDIENTS

2 cups (230 g) blueberries
2 cups (500 mL) Champagne
vinegar or apple cider vinegar
½ cup (85 g) granulated sugar
½ teaspoon grated orange peel

Blueberry vinegar makes a nice gift when presented in a decorative bottle.

Wash blueberries and pat dry. Heat vinegar with sugar in nonaluminum saucepan, stirring until sugar is dissolved; do not boil. Gently stir in blueberries and orange peel. Pour into bottle and let stand 10 days at room temperature. Taste vinegar; if sufficiently flavored, strain off blueberries and pour vinegar into a sterilized bottle. If necessary, let vinegar stand for a longer time, tasting every day or two, until well flavored.

Rice vinegar is mild and goes best with Oriental noodle dishes and neutral greens.

Combine vinegar, garlic, ginger and cilantro. Pour into bottle and let stand at room temperature for 10 to 14 days. Strain, discarding garlic, ginger and cilantro. Pour vinegar into a sterilized bottle.

ORIENTAL VINEGAR

MAKES 2 CUPS (500 mL)

INGREDIENTS

2 cups (500 mL) Japanese
rice vinegar
2 cloves garlic
2 slices peeled fresh ginger
2 or 3 sprigs cilantro

LIME THYME VINEGAR

MAKES 2 CUPS (500 mL)

INGREDIENTS

2 cups (500 mL) white
wine vinegar
zest of 1 lime
8 sprigs fresh thyme
1 clove garlic

Try this sprightly combination with tossed greens and in fish or vegetable salads.

Combine vinegar, lime zest, thyme and garlic. Pour into a bottle and let stand at room temperature for about 2 weeks. Strain and discard zest, herbs and garlic. Pour vinegar into a sterilized bottle, adding a sprig of thyme.

OILS

The oil is the basis for any salad dressing, and there are lots of choices. Included are recipes for flavoring specialty oils.

KINDS OF OIL

Olive oil comes in several different grades. Oil from the first pressing, **extra virgin**, *is the most expensive. Only the choicest olives are used and no heat is employed to extract the oil. It has little sediment and low acidity.*

The second pressing is **virgin olive oil**. *It has a slight amount of sediment and 1.5 to 5 percent acidity. Heat and high pressure are applied to the olives to extract the oil.*

Pure olive oil *is made from the third pressing of the olives under heat. More expensive olive oils are often added for better flavor. The product is designated "pure" because it contains only oil from olives.*

Most olive oil comes from the Mediterranean countries, where the olives are picked from trees that can be several hundred years old. Italian olive oil is rich, with a full olive flavor and a deep green color. French olive oil is lighter in color and has a more delicate, fruity flavor. Spanish olive oil has a strong, assertive flavor and is dark green. Greek olive oil is usually thicker than the others, but it has a lighter flavor. In recent years, California-grown olives are also being pressed into oil, but supplies are limited.

The best way to choose an olive oil for salad is to buy it in small quantities and try it. Many people find that an assertive oil masks the flavor of the other ingredients, especially delicate salad greens. Others like the way it tones down the vinegar. It's a matter of taste and pocketbook.

Here are some other oils to use in salads; they can be substituted for olive oil in a one-to-one ratio. Like olive oil, these contain no cholesterol.

Almond oil *is expensive and hard to find, but its delicate, fresh almond flavor gives a lift to vegetable salads. Finish off the dish with a few toasted almond slivers.*

Avocado oil *New from California, this is easy to digest but has little flavor of its own.*

Grapeseed oil *is a byproduct of the*

French wine industry. Light and aromatic, it is often blended with olive oil and herbs.

Hazelnut oil *is expensive and hard to find, but it gives an unexpected nutty flavor to greens and to meat salads.*

Walnut oil *Most is imported from France. Try it on poultry and spinach salads along with a few toasted walnuts on top.*

Peanut oil *has a bland taste; it's generally used when you don't want the flavor of the oil to penetrate the salad ingredients.*

Vegetable oils *are light and often bland-tasting oils made from vegetables and seeds such as corn, cottonseed, soybean and safflower. When the label says "pure" it contains only one kind of oil, but more often vegetable oils are a blend of several types.*

HERB OIL

MAKES 1¾ CUPS (425 mL)

INGREDIENTS

1 cup (60 g) fresh herb sprigs
(parsley, tarragon, thyme, sage,
rosemary, basil)
¼ teaspoon black peppercorns
1¾ cups (425 mL) olive oil

Try this on any green or vegetable salad, or for making mayonnaise.

Wash herbs and gently pat dry. Place herbs and peppercorns in a pint jar or bottle and add olive oil. Store in a dark spot for 10 days. Strain oil and discard herbs. Return oil to bottle and add a sprig or two of fresh herbs.

Opposite: Garden Salad with Fennel Vinaigrette
(p. 52)

This peppered olive oil gives a zippy flavor to seafood, pasta and green salads.

Place chili pepper, garlic, bay leaves and peppercorns in bottom of a clean pint jar or bottle. Slowly pour in olive oil. Cover and let stand for several days before using. Strain oil and store in clean bottle.

PEPPERED OLIVE OIL

MAKES 2 CUPS (500 mL)

INGREDIENTS

1 small dried red chili pepper
2 cloves garlic
2 bay leaves
6 peppercorns
2 cups (500 mL) olive oil

81

Opposite: Baked Goat Cheese with Tomato-Mint Dressing (p. 61)

GINGER-GARLIC OIL

MAKES 2 CUPS (500 mL)

INGREDIENTS

4 slices fresh ginger, ¼ inch
(.5 cm) thick
4 cloves garlic
1 shallot, sliced
1¾ cups (425 mL) peanut oil
¼ cup (60 mL) sesame oil

With a hint of ginger and garlic, use this oil in chicken salads, fish salads and stir-fried dishes.

Place ginger, garlic and shallot slices in a clean pint jar or bottle. Slowly pour in oils. Cover and let stand for several days before using. Strain oil and store in clean bottle.

A flavorful oil with green salads or taco salads, or in any Mexican dish.

Place cilantro, chili pepper, cumin seeds, oregano and garlic in the bottom of a clean pint jar. Cover with olive oil and let stand 1 week. Strain oil and store in clean bottle.

TEX-MEX OIL

MAKES 2 CUPS (500 mL)

INGREDIENTS

4 sprigs cilantro
1 dried chili pepper
½ teaspoon cumin seeds
2 sprigs fresh oregano
2 cloves garlic
2 cups (500 mL) olive oil

CONSTRUCT YOUR OWN SALADS

Here's a rundown on salad greens, the ones we all know and some of the newer choices. Included are six salad dressings so you can become creative in composing your own salads.

SALAD GREENS—A RUNDOWN

Arugula has dark green, notched leaves with a peppery or mustardy tang. It is also called roquette or rocket and has been popular in Italy since Roman days.

Belgian endive's firm, slender leaves are creamy white with pale yellow tips. It is slightly bitter in flavor.

Butter lettuce is a head lettuce with a buttery texture, delicate flavor. Its inner leaves are pale butter color; the outer leaves are medium green.

Frisee: This is baby chicory. Its slightly bitter, spiked leaves range from almost white to light green.

Green leaf lettuce has crisp, tender, loose leaves and a delicate flavor.

Green oak leaf is baby lettuce with lobed green leaves. It has a sharper flavor than red oak leaf.

Iceberg lettuce is a head lettuce with a crisp texture and mild flavor.

Lolla rossa is crinkly baby leaf lettuce with rosy tips.

Mâche, with its teardrop-shaped dark green leaves, grows in rosette clusters.

It has a delicate texture with a subtle, nutty flavor. It is also called corn salad or lamb's lettuce.

Mesclun is a popular French mixture of six or more baby lettuces that are grown in rows next to each other and harvested at the same time. The varieties combine tastes, textures, and colors.

Radicchio has small, round heads that range in color from purplish red to variegated leaves with white ribs. It has a bitter flavor. It usually is imported from Italy and is expensive.

Red leaf lettuce is similar to green leaf lettuce, but the tips of its leaves range from red to bronze.

Red oak leaf is baby lettuce with deeply cut, finely divided leaves very similar to oak leaves, but with more ruffled edges and burgundy centers.

Romaine is a perennial favorite because of its lasting crunchiness and mild flavor. It is traditionally used in Caesar salad and is also called cos lettuce.

Watercress: Dark green, peppery-flavored leaves add a tang to milder greens.

Made with part-skim yogurt, a tablespoon of this dressing has less than 10 calories. Spoon over tossed greens or chicken or fish salads.

Combine yogurt, cucumber, green and red peppers, scallions, dill, parsley, lime juice, salt and pepper. Stir well. Chill 30 minutes before serving.

LOW-CALORIE VEGGIE SALAD DRESSING

MAKES 1½ CUPS (360 mL)

INGREDIENTS

1 cup (240 mL) plain yogurt
½ cucumber, peeled,
seeded, grated
1 tablespoon finely chopped
green pepper
1 tablespoon finely chopped
red pepper
2 scallions, chopped
1 tablespoon chopped fresh dill
1 tablespoon chopped
fresh parsley
1 tablespoon fresh lime juice
salt and pepper to taste

BUTTERMILK SALAD DRESSING

MAKES 2 CUPS (500 mL)

INGREDIENTS

1 cup (240 mL) buttermilk
1 cup (240 mL) mayonnaise,
preferably homemade
2 tablespoons chopped
Italian parsley
1 teaspoon chopped fresh basil
1 teaspoon chopped
fresh oregano
1 teaspoon chopped
fresh rosemary
1 tablespoon chopped
fresh shallots
salt and pepper to taste

Buttermilk lends a slight tang to this herbal dressing, good on green and vegetable salads.

Combine buttermilk and mayonnaise with fork. Stir in parsley, basil, oregano, rosemary and shallots. Season with salt and pepper.

Pick and choose a combination of peaches, pears, plums, grapes, apples, or orange or grapefruit sections to toss with this dressing. Add strawberries and raspberries just before serving so they do not discolor the mixture.

In a saucepan combine honey, pineapple juice, cornstarch, lime juice and grated peels. Simmer 5 minutes, then let cool. Add fruit and marinate for 30 minutes before serving.

FRUIT SALAD DRESSING

MAKES ABOUT 1 CUP (240 mL)

INGREDIENTS

½ cup (120 mL) honey
½ cup (120 mL) pineapple juice
2 tablespoons cornstarch
1 tablespoon fresh lime juice
1 teaspoon grated lemon peel
1 teaspoon grated orange peel
fruit, cut or sectioned
as necessary

LEMON SALAD DRESSING

MAKES ABOUT 1 CUP (240 mL)

INGREDIENTS

2 teaspoons grated lemon peel
¼ cup (60 mL) fresh
lemon juice
⅔ cup (160 mL) olive oil
1 shallot, finely chopped
salt and pepper to taste
½ teaspoon dry mustard
½ teaspoon paprika
½ teaspoon ground coriander
¼ teaspoon ground celery seed
hot pepper sauce to taste

Lemon lovers will go for this dressing on fish and chicken salads.

Whisk together lemon peel, lemon juice, olive oil, shallot, salt, pepper, dry mustard, paprika, coriander, celery seed and pepper sauce. Chill well before serving.

This dressing tastes best with fresh herbs. Use it on simple green salads.

Whisk together the olive oil, vinegar, garlic, shallot, parsley, basil, thyme, capers, anchovies, salt and pepper.

PROVENÇAL SALAD DRESSING

MAKES 1¼ CUPS (300 mL)

INGREDIENTS

¾ cup (180 mL) French olive oil
¼ cup (60 mL) red wine vinegar
2 cloves garlic, put through
garlic press
1 shallot, finely chopped
2 tablespoons finely chopped
Italian parsley
1 tablespoon chopped basil
1 tablespoon chopped thyme
1 tablespoon capers, rinsed
and drained
2 anchovy fillets, mashed
salt and pepper to taste

Croutons can be tossed into any main-dish green or vegetable salad.

Method 1.

Cut bread into ½-inch (1-cm) cubes. Heat oil or butter in a heavy skillet, add bread cubes and sauté until golden brown, stirring constantly.

Method 2.

Brush bread with oil or melted butter and cut into ½-inch (1-cm) cubes. Place on a cookie sheet and bake in a preheated 400°F (200°C) oven for 10 to 15 minutes or until crisp and golden, shaking the pan once or twice during baking to turn cubes.

Flavoring

While croutons are still hot, sprinkle with chili powder, curry powder, garlic powder, dried thyme or Parmesan cheese.

CROUTONS

SERVES 6

INGREDIENTS

6 slices day-old bread
6 tablespoons olive oil or
butter flavoring

INDEX

93

FAVORITE RECIPES

Marie Bianco is a food writer with Newsday. *She is the author of three other Barron's books,* 32 Seafood Dishes, 32 Fabulous Cookies, *and* Wild about Potatoes.

This book is for Sarah Marie Falvey, who has managed to bring so much joy into so many lives in such a short time.
And a special thanks to Pat Connell for a first-rate job of editing, and to Grace Freedson and Carolyn Horne of Barron's for their guidance.